A CUP OF MINDFULNESS

FOR THE BUSY & RESTLESS

Fast, Simple Ways to Improve Your Focus

BY LISA BÉLANGER, PHD

Published by ConsciousWorks Consulting Inc
Canmore, Alberta, Canada
consciousworks.co

ISBN: ISBN 978-1-7770907-0-8

Book design by Dean Pickup CanadaBookDesign.com

Printed in Canada

TABLE OF CONTENTS

This book is for Maxwell & Aurora

Thank you for keeping me present

Thank you so much to my friends and family that took the time to read and review the book. I cannot tell you how much I value your thoughts, ideas, and insight. Thank you my editor, Gillian Buckley and my designer, Dean Pickup.

INTRODUCTION

The Power of the Mind

"Reading is just humans staring
at dead trees, hallucinating." – Anonymous

C an you control what you are paying attention
to? As you are reading this book, can you draw
your attention to what you can hear? The sensation
of what is touching your skin, from your clothes to
your feet on the floor? Can you notice your breath?
If you get distracted, are you able to bring yourself
back to the words on the page and their meaning?

Perhaps more relatable: when you are dealing
with a difficult person, can you remain calm and
draw a solution even when they seem unreasonable?

When you get bored while working and automatically check social media, are you able to notice and bring yourself back? Are you able to keep your mind focused on the big test, big game, big presentation without being drawn into distractions? Speaking of the big moments, are you able to stay present and fully experience them or do you get overcome with anxiety and fear? When you are lying in bed and you find your mind racing from worry to negative thoughts to useless thoughts, can you stop the racing and clear your mind?

The power of your mind is that you can imagine the world as it is not. We spend approximately 46.9% of our time thinking about the future or the past,[1] neither of which are our current reality. Thinking of the past or the future *can* serve us sometimes when strategizing or allowing us to learn from past events, however most of the time it takes us from living in the moment, decreases our performance and takes us far from the life we desire to live.

You can either be controlled by your thoughts or control your thoughts. Think about that—have you ever been consumed with thoughts that are not serving you in any way? When this was described to me, this example stuck in my mind: you are speaking in front of a group of people and you see two people at the back of the room whispering, looking at you, and then laughing.

You have a choice: you can think to yourself "they are laughing at me because of something bad" and become self-conscious and even go down a spiral of what they could be talking about or criticizing.

Or

You could think to yourself "they are really engaged with the content. They're enjoying it and relating it to something funny."

Chances are you will never know why they are laughing. By choosing to believe the first option, you will more likely negatively impact your performance and make yourself feel terrible.

Believing the second option could give you energy and positively impact your performance, even boost your confidence.

While I was writing this book, I was travelling to

the eastern US from western Canada and it was the first trip away from my youngest child. I was already having a hard time with the trip, and then there was bad news after bad news—flight delays, missed connections, and a travel time of over twenty hours. I was sitting in the airport lounge, feeling frustrated, a little sorry for myself and cursing my flight choices and several major airlines.

My friend from Australia (the only friend awake at this time) offered this reframe: he said as far as I can see it, you are in a quiet, private lounge (it was so late there were no other passengers) where no one needs or wants you. It is peaceful and you have wine.

We were looking at the exact same situation but having two different responses. The choice is entirely in your control: you just need to have the awareness of your thoughts and the skills to guide them when they are no longer serving your best interests.

How many times do you stay awake at night with doubt, worry, frustrations, etc.? Or you are all consumed with thoughts that impact a presentation or the big game? Or you don't act for fear of rejection? All of these are our constructed realities: WE design them and then let the reality we design become our lives.

In work and in life it is your competitive advantage to be able to control where your mind is at any given time. Not only does mindfulness help you design a reality that serves you and your interests, but it also helps you develop key components of leadership such as emotional intelligence and resilience. Mindfulness training (whatever it may be called) is now a key component of any leadership training worth a damn.

The problem is that mindfulness requires practice. It requires repetitive deliberate action to be able to shift your attention and focus, and yet we are not usually taught how to do it. It can also be daunting to add yet another thing to an already busy schedule.

To make things even more complex, for those whom the practice would most benefit, it can be a very challenging and frustrating experience. Here, I use myself as an example—I run a company, operations of a national charity, have two small children and would like to see my husband and friends on occasion. I barely have time to go to the washroom. If someone was to tell me to fit in a half-hour practice, I would laugh at them, even though I know all the benefits. At this time, it just isn't feasible. (Note: practicing meditation while using the bathroom is a great way to fit it in. The RPM morning routine: rise, pee, meditate.)

Acknowledging both the lack of time and the value of mindfulness, what I am proposing in this book is not to add something else to your schedule (if you can, great! If not, join the club!). I am talking about short practices that will have an impact, even when life gets chaotic. Instead of giving you another "you should be doing…" I am hoping to give you a "here is a way to do the same, while keeping your sanity."

WHAT IS MINDFULNESS?

Mindfulness is a way of doing things vs having things to do.

It is small practices that will end up saving your time, energy, and effort but allow you to slow down, make better decisions, decrease anxiety, improve health and give you a bit more sanity. Making a small effort to create habits doing the things we already do daily will have a large, far reaching impact.

Mindfulness vs Meditation

These terms often get used interchangeably and I understand the confusion given one of the most common types of meditation discussed is *mindful meditation*.

Meditation: any act or practice you are choosing to do good for yourself involving contemplation or reflection.

Now there are countless definitions of meditation; this is the one I choose to use. Meditation is a set of practices that involve active reflection on one's experience, which can include activities such as journaling, body scans, progressive relaxation, and yoga or mental exercises that can include repeated chanting or repetitive mantras.

Mindfulness: the state of being conscious or aware. You are living mindfully when you are actively aware of where your attention is, and typically it means that your awareness is on the present. Basically, being present.

Mindful meditation is the dedicated act of practicing your awareness.

What is being discussed in this book is mindful meditation lite. Practicing where your awareness is and, without judgment, noticing when you are distracted and bringing your thoughts back to where you are intending to place your attention. The practices described in this book are short. For added benefit try longer durations. More important than duration for long term practice is consistency. Start small and do what you can to fit it into your life.

To be clear, a short mindful practice per day is better than none at all. That is the first step. Longer is better.

While we are throwing around terms, you may have heard of Mindfulness Based Stress Reduction (MBSR). This is the most common meditation or mindfulness strategy used in medical and psychological research. This is usually a skill set taught over six or eight weeks and involves many of the practices discussed in this book and others, such as guided meditations and progressive relaxation.

It also teaches how to use techniques when cued by stress indicators or known stressful events. If you are curious about these techniques, there are numerous courses offered both in person in the community or online. Some programs have a cost, and many are free. I have included a few options on the resource website.

Confession: I Am Not a Yoga Teacher

I am not a yoga teacher (although I do enjoy the practice, regardless of how much I look like a robot trying to touch my toes), nor have I ever lived at a monastery. I came upon mindfulness out of necessity as I was completing my graduate research. I am an expert in behaviour change and exercise. My studies during my degrees were focused on the impact of exercise on the mental and physical well-being of cancer patients and survivors. Meditation and mindfulness kept coming up in the journals I was reading and the conferences I was attending.

It was certainly not the first time I had heard of mindfulness and meditation, but it was not something I understood or, to be frank, was even remotely curious about. Mindfulness…that was fine for other people. I was a type AAA personality, a "control enthusiast" and a "true" scientist of things I could measure and experience. Mindfulness and meditation seemed, for a lack of better word, "woo-woo."

The studies did offer insight into topics cancer patients and survivors were curious about: an effective alternative to pain medication and the ability to decrease the fear of cancer reoccurrence. These were certainly real issues, and it made me dive into the scientific studies further. There was no denying the depth and breadth of the research on mindfulness well beyond the cancer field. If I deemed myself someone who makes decisions based on evidence, there was simply no way I could deny the benefit of these techniques. Benefits included everything from stress management and treatment of PTSD, to attention, focus and work performance. They were all things I would benefit from extensively.

I knew there was simply no way I could immediately engage with longer meditations. The idea of sitting still or being alone with my thoughts was both terrifying and above and beyond what I could imagine. Logistically, this idea is flawed. I simply did not have enough time. I was completing my PhD and working three jobs on top of school. So I settled on the simple practice of mindfully drinking my coffee every morning. I absolutely love coffee: the taste, the smell, the routine that accompanies it. What if I didn't start to work, mentally plan out my day, or overthink the latest challenge and instead just drank my coffee?

This is one of the key elements to successfully changing a behaviour. Start small.

The idea is simple: only drink your coffee and come to your five senses. What does the preparing and pouring of the coffee sound like? What does it smell like? What does it look like? What is the colour and texture? What does it feel like on your tongue and as it goes down your esophagus? What does it taste like? Where are those tastes experienced on your tongue? Just drink your coffee with awareness.

I started this practice about four years ago at a time where I was finishing my PhD, starting a national charity, starting a new relationship and moving. There was no way I could predict what the next four years would have in store and how much this simple act completely changed my ability to cope, manage and perform. I started this practice out of curiosity. I continued it because I looked forward to the quiet moment. I maintained it because of enjoyment and perceived benefit.

My daily coffee routine is a simple practice, and it can be a gateway to longer, more in-depth practices. Over the past years it is what I have maintained in the most chaotic parts of life.

This simple cup of mindfulness is the reason for my sanity, the quality of my relationships, my decision making, why I don't yell at difficult people and why I deserve a goddamn cape for the ability to rise and do what is seemingly impossible.

Why Am I Writing This Book?

For years now I have been finding myself constantly frustrated and feeling helpless to the number of people—friends, family, patients—who have crippling stress, burnout, depression or anxiety. During my career I have had the honour of speaking with people as they walk through the hardest part of their lives, face their biggest obstacles and even confront their mortality.

I have had to say many sentences I never thought I would have to say over the past couple of years and face seemingly impossible situations. Whether it be giving a eulogy, climbing Kilimanjaro, dealing with difficult people, falling in love, losing a job, going through a health crisis or navigating parenting—and let's be honest it is never just one of these things at a time—awareness is key to successfully navigating these situations. You cannot control your situation, but you can control your response.

I became passionate about what we could do to help guide us through life, while keeping our ability to perform at our best, and experience and enjoy life. Given my "control enthusiast" personality, my question became "what do we have within our control that could help our mental strength?"

It always came back to the idea of the M&Ms— mindfulness and movement. Your body benefits from movement; your mind benefits from stillness. Both behaviours are in our control, are free and have dramatic impact on our brain structure, chemistry and our thoughts and behaviours.

Your Competitive Advantage

We are told to "pay attention" dating back to grade school, but most of us are not *taught* how to pay attention. Our attention (a.k.a. where our awareness goes) is our currency. We give our attention in exchange for a paycheque and it is what we have to give our relationships, our passion and to ourselves. As such, learning how to spend your attention is the first thing you will learn if you step into a psychologist's office no matter your rationale for walking in the door.

We don't need to wait for a crisis to start the practice. It is a coping skill, nay, the *best* coping skill to have in your arsenal before you need it. While you can start a mindfulness practice anytime, I suggest starting while things are in your control, so the routine is second nature for you when you need it the most. If I could give a gift to the people around me it would be this— the ability to slow down when needed, to experience the present and to relieve the worry, fear and dread that is only available when thinking about the future or the past.

There is the corny saying "now is a gift, that is why they call it the present."

commence eye rolling

But it truly is.

When teaching a mindfulness session with business leaders in Banff, Canada, I had one young leader raise his hand and bring up what I think everyone was thinking, but almost no one said: "Why be present when everyone in the room got to the positions of leadership that they are in today by being able to strategize about the future and learn from the past?"

Well, I'm glad he asked.

The skills and advantages that comes with practice is to be able to focus your attention on the future, the past and the present when it serves you. We spend the majority of our day unconsciously slipping from future to present to past and often with no intent, and no benefit. A great example is lying in bed ruminating on perceived risk or spending time and energy on what your neighbours meant when they said something to you the other day. To be conscious of what your thoughts are, to be able to direct them to where you want them to go—that is the advantage! Even brief meditation improves attention.[2]

There is value for both life and business to be able to look to the past and future. Learning and living mindfully is the ability to switch to the present and live there when it is beneficial—and then switch your awareness to the past or future when the situation calls for it. It is when we become trapped in either the future or the past that things can become problematic. A potential cause or amplifier of depression is said to be living in the past. Anxiety, on the other hand, can be worsened by living in the future.

When you are in a strategy meeting, yes of course your mind will be thinking of a year, five years, ten years in the future. When you are having

your monthly meeting to review your business
metrics you will be thinking about past days, months
and years. But when you are lying in bed trying
to fall asleep there is no advantage to be thinking
about any of it. When you are having a conversation
with your child or spouse, there is no purpose to be
anywhere else but present (put down your phone,
you won't regret it). As I will talk about later on in
the book, there is no such thing as multi-tasking,
there is just doing two things poorly.

Don't Say Mindfulness

One of my keynotes shares the same name as this
book. I have been asked several times to give
mindfulness presentations or workshops without using
the word *mindfulness*. Some people lean away from
the word (and to be fair, I was one of them) thinking it
is great...for other people or for monks and yogis.

And don't you dare say mental health.

From my experience, the exact same thing is
true using the term mental health. We have confused
mental health and mental illness so much that when

we talk about mental health, at least half the room checks out, thinking it is not relevant to them.

WE. ALL. HAVE. MENTAL HEALTH.

A colleague of mine was telling me about a speaker he had invited to his oil and gas company, where the majority of the audience was male and engineers. The speaker asked the audience two questions and asked them to raise their hands to acknowledge the answer.

1. Who here has suffered mental distress or mental illness at some point in their life?

2. Who here has sh!t their pants in public?

Guess which one more of the audience admitted too? Hint: it required more laundry. This is, of course, statistically incorrect. We have all suffered from a mentally distressful situation, and yet the conversation is still not open.

Often when I speak about mental health, I call it brain health as it is the EXACT SAME THING.

Every thought we have produces a chemical and neurological response in your brain. Every change in brain chemistry has the potential to change your thoughts and responding behaviours. We often separate mental and physical health, and yet they are so intertwined they are impossible to separate.

Do you know what the number one (as in first or "go to") treatment for any psychological condition is? Physical activity. The research is undeniable. Physical activity impacts our moods, thoughts, stress and resulting behaviour.

The number one treatment getting the most research attention for both preventing and treating Alzheimer's? Physical activity.

Your health encompasses your whole body, whether illness is expressed through thoughts and behaviours or pain and sores. What we do to prevent most illnesses is taking care of our movement, mind/stress, sleep and what we eat.

Brain health. We all have it. We all need to be proactive about it. End of rant.

The same thing is true with our minds (or mindfulness): it should be something we are all discussing and yet, we don't.

When I ask a group what they think of when they think about *mindfulness*, the most common answers I get are (and I kid you not) 1) some version of a monk, cross legged on top of a mountain and 2) yoga pants.

The whole discussion about mindfulness can be replaced by "attention management" or "focus training" and deliver the same impact. If these are terms you are more comfortable with then read the rest of the content with those substitutes. Hell, call it "magic" for all I care, just try to lift any preconceived notions of what mindfulness is and who it is for.

Mindfulness is the practice of bringing our thoughts back to what we would like to be thinking about in a non-judgmental way. We all need it. We all need to be proactive about it.

Practice Matters

Did I notice any differences in my life with such a small and short practice as drinking my coffee mindfully? Now this is anecdotal evidence, but yes. I noticed more where my thoughts and attention were spent during the day. I did notice my desire and ability to be in the present instead of letting my mind wander to the past or to the future in unproductive ways (worrying, ruminating). I also started to become more curious about other practices, longer (albeit still under fifteen minutes) meditations or breathing exercises.

Where the benefits smacked me in the face and became undeniable to me is when my husband and I lost four family members in three and a half weeks. It was a blur of survival while we travelled over 36,000 km back and forth across the country to funerals...with a two-year-old. (To give perspective the circumference of the world is 40,000 km.) It was incredibly stressful, devoid of sleep and surrounded by grief at every stop. I have never been more physically and emotionally drained.

The morning after my husband's grandfather's funeral in Niagara, we arrived at Pearson Airport in Toronto. When we finally got through security and I arrived at the gate I looked up to my husband and noticed that he was absolutely drained. It was to a level I had never seen before. I did the only thing I could think of doing: I got him a very large coffee. Out of habit, I put the wallet on the stroller.

Now the thing is, we were not going to the same destination. My husband and my son were heading back to Calgary, Alberta: home. I was over 5000 kms away to St. John's, Newfoundland, to host a cancer retreat for the national charity that I operate that provides wellness programming to cancer survivors. While I slowed down or delegated the things I could, the world was still spinning, and I needed to be there.

Moments after handing the coffee to my husband, the announcement was made for their flight. My husband, son and the stroller took off to Calgary. I wandered over to the St. John's gate and sat down. My mom called and asked how we were holding up. I responded: "twenty minutes at a time and naïve optimism." As I was speaking to her, I was searching through my purse for my wallet. I slowly realized what had happened. I paused and said "the next twenty minutes just got interesting. I don't have my wallet."

I walked towards the gate agent and was surprised I did not feel the physiological response to stress. You know the feeling—your heart races, you start to sweat, your mouth gets dry. Nothing. I remained solution focused.

I explained what had happened and I got to see *her* physiological response to stress.

You have no money?

No.

No ID?

No.

Is there anyone who can bring you some documentation?

No, I am not from here.

So, you have no money?

Still no.

Now before I started practicing mindfulness, I know exactly what would have happened. I would have sworn, sat down and looked around Pearson airport thinking "well, I guess this is my home now."

I completely attribute the practice to my being able to start at the present and think through the problem at hand even when exhausted.

To be continued...

The Brain, the Data and my Skepticism

Part of my skepticism on mindfulness came from the fact that you could not see the changes occurring and the potential changes seemed so abstract. In contrast, when you exercise you can not only feel changes but see them. You have confirmation you did the practice by getting sweaty, having flushed cheeks and a rapid beating heart and feeling like you worked your muscles (immediate feedback). With time and continuous practice, you see changes in your body whether it is muscle definition or decrease in your blood pressure (delayed feedback). In the case of mindfulness, the difference is in your brain, how it operates, and new neural connections are unseen.

I am not saying I want to see sparks and rainbows coming from my head when I practice (all right, that would be validating) but it would be nice to have some measurable results to indicate my time and energy investment into this practice created a return.

The Science of Mindfulness

This is where the science and brain imaging come in for me. The results are staggering, and by that I mean if there was a drug that could produce even half of these results, it would be prescribed to everyone.

Note: there are some current technologies that can aid if you are the immediate feedback kind of person. Products such as MUSE, a headband you wear that measures your brain waves and works with your smartphone to give you real time feedback, provides a data capture after each meditation session and gamifies the experience.

For ease, I will be describing what happens in the brain during mindfulness meditation—the deliberate practice of mindfulness. The changes discussed are the result of varying lengths of practice both in session duration and the number of sessions. Two things remain true, the longer you practice (duration), the greater the impact, up to about an hour/day (longer durations are not typically studied) and the greater the frequency that you practice, the greater the benefit.

Stress and Reactions

MRI scans show that after just eight weeks of practice, the amygdala (or our brain's fight or flight centre) shrinks. This is the primal part of our brain which is responsible for emotion and triggering our stress response.

While the amygdala is shrinking, the prefrontal cortex, the part of the brain associated with higher level processes such as awareness, concentration and decision making, becomes more neurologically dense. This means that we can handle more stress before a reaction such as fight or flight and can recruit a more thoughtful response.

Another way that mindfulness impacts our ability to react is that during mindfulness we breathe more deeply (especially during breath exercises) allowing the brain to receive more oxygen. When we do not properly oxygenate the brain, our executive function and memory are the first to be impacted impeding our ability to reflect and respond.

Changing our brain's response to stress has a cascading impact on our bodies by reducing blood biomarkers for stress and inflammation (i.e., C-reactive proteins, interleukin 6 and cortisol) which are associated with illness and disease.

Your Brain Needs an Off Switch

For your brain to function at its best, it needs rest. This means a variety of activities such as sleep, play/enjoyment, safety and connection to name a few. To be fair, rest may not be the right word as your brain is more active when you are asleep than awake. Recovery may be the best way to think about it. Being able to practice mindfulness allows for better work (better productivity, focus, creativity, decision making, etc.) and it also helps you recover better. It helps you get to sleep when your mind is racing, it can help you disconnect from work or stress, and it helps you connect better to those around you and with yourself.

Much like most things in nature (e.g., seasons, circadian rhythms, menstruation) our brains have cycles. They need disconnection as much as they might try to stay engaged with other ideas.

> Get rid of the stigma of doing nothing—it is one of the best things you can do for yourself.

We talk often in sports, business, and school about work ethic, resilience, grit—this is not possible long term without effective recovery. Even when rest periods are short, say a quiet drive to pick up your kids, the space between meetings/classes/clients, waiting for the doctor's appointment or driving (note: don't completely turn off while driving, keep your eyes open and on task just let all the other stuff go), offer the space and time for recovery.

Human brains need recovery time. Mindfulness can help you do this, quickly and effectively. Find a time. Do it.

BENEFITS OF MINDFULNESS

Here are just some of the benefits of meditation.

Pain Relief

An odd thing is observed when researchers scan the brains of meditators experiencing pain. Areas of the brain that are associated with pain are more active (usually meaning a greater experience of pain) and yet meditators report experiencing less pain. The meditators also experience a large decrease in activity in regions of the brain involved in appraising stimuli, memory and emotion, meaning that we pass less automatic judgment on our experience. While these two parts of the brain are normally functionally connected, through practice they consciously separate allowing for meditators to experience less pain.

Keeps Your Brain Young

As we age, like the rest of our bodies, our brains deteriorate. The result can be seen in things such as lost keys, difficulty organizing multiple projects or completing complex tasks. This is known as age related cognitive decline. This decline however, is not inevitable. The way our brains age can be influenced by factors such as our diet, physical activity, and education.[3]

In order to keep your mind sharp, you must keep your brain's mental capacity in working order. As discussed above, meditation influences both the brain's structures and the way they connect, which can increase the brain's efficiency in acting thoughtfully, strategically and with intention. In addition, a study at UCLA found that in meditators the regions of the brain most affected by cognitive decline and aging were more neurologically dense.[4]

For even the greatest skeptics, the evidence is accumulating at such a rapid and robust rate that it becomes impossible to look the other way. If you are one of those "oh, but it doesn't/won't work for me" types—either because you believe it is beyond you or your mind is so scattered—I feel it is my duty to tell you, you are not so special (she says lovingly). The largest barrier to mindfulness is that must be practiced often for a dedicated amount of time, but, believe me, it is worth every moment of investment.

How to Practice

The ability to practice mindfulness has the potential to impact every aspect of life. While you could initially start the practice with a specific reason that is meaningful to you (for example, to increase performance at work as you overcome the challenge of shorter days due to the addition of a newborn at home), the practice can later have a whole different purpose, for example dealing with grief of a loved one or dealing with the uncertainty of a diagnosis.

The list below is certainly not all inclusive and how and when mindfulness is impactful for you may change. Your purpose of practice may change or your desire to teach this to others (such as helping your child navigate test anxiety, an experience you never personally had) may be beyond your scope of imagination now.

In this short book, I don't have the space to go through the effects of mindfulness on specific medical conditions such as anxiety, insomnia, obsessive-compulsive disorder, panic attacks, post-traumatic stress disorder, cancer, heart disease, pregnancy, addiction and the list goes on. Why did I leave these well researched findings from this section? The main reason is that I wanted this book to be a short introduction and not everyone deals with these conditions while everyone will go through the list below. Also the science around mindfulness and the above conditions is so rapidly progressing that a web search would offer more up to date information. I will say this: in short, mindfulness is good for anyone experiencing any kind of medical concern— physical or mental. Research, or ask your health care providers for more specific information. There are often classes or groups specific to medical conditions which can offer up to date information, social support and guidance.

If these groups are not available locally, check online. There are thousands of online courses to fit your desired outcome, your schedule, your curiosity level and learning style.

...for Performance

I have mentioned several times already why having a mindfulness practice and being aware of your thoughts can offer you a competitive advantage. From being able to focus and get more done with the time you have, becoming a successful uni-tasker (perform one task at a time), being more creative, decreasing error rate and developing emotional intelligence, the impact of a mindfulness practice has not only a place in the corporate world but is a foundation to every kind of work from knowledge work to call centres to factory lines.

The companies that have decided that mindfulness training is worth the investment is growing exponentially and includes large corporations such as General Mills, Apple, Google, and Nike with more and more employers offering mindfulness training.

The reason many of the companies invest in mind-fulness is simply the impact to their bottom line: reduced health care costs, decreased sick leaves and fewer stressed out employees improve productivity.

When I work with corporate clients, often it is with their leadership. I teach similar simple yet effective practices such as those found in this book with the purpose of fitting them into an already busy day. This is different from ongoing meditation training which most companies opt into through having meditation teachers come to their office, offering access to different apps or technology, or providing meditation rooms.

Regardless of the level of teaching and support, one of the most interesting and effective uses I hear about is using short practices to separate one's day. For example, using a short practice before having a hard conversation with your spouse. It could also be useful after having a difficult conversation with an employee before stepping into a strategy meeting. It is best to leave the thoughts and feelings of the conversation in your office before you step into a board meeting.

If you are a sports fan, you may have noticed that mindfulness and meditation are getting a lot of hype in recent years. Athletes like tennis phenom Bianca Andreescu, basketball player LeBron James and the entire Seattle Seahawks NFL team have gone on record to say meditation is a key to their success.

If you are someone on a stage—whether that be professional sports, giving presentations at work, or standing up for something you believe in—it is an advantage to be able to stay in the moment and not become distracted by what is going on outside the playing field.

...for Grief

Grief of any sort can have a profound impact on everything from cognition to your sleep. Grief from the loss of a loved one is considered a severe psychological stressor that can trigger a variety of mental and physical disorders. We will all go through immense grief at some point, and while it is one of the most intense human emotions, the only way past it, is through it. What mindfulness can do is help your awareness to ensure you are able to feel what you need to go through the experience.

After a loss (even if you have not practiced before), something called mindfulness-based cognitive therapy, which is a combination of cognitive behavioural therapy and mindfulness, can help reduce feelings of grief, trouble with emotional regulation, depression and anxiety.[5] This requires a psychologist (go get one, they are incredible, mine is Barbara) but having a base to understand and practice mindfulness will significantly help.

While I don't wish grief on anyone, it is unfortunately inevitable for us all as one of the sad guarantees in life. Mindfulness is a small gift to help you through these difficult times. As mentioned, there is no way around, just through.

...for Transition and Uncertainty

So much of life is uncertain. It is what makes it both wonderful and anxiety provoking. Even "certain" things are not certain. The intolerance or fear of uncertainty can interfere with problem solving and lead people to do impulsive behaviours to avoid uncertainty, which doesn't necessarily solve the problem. The inability to stay calm when faced with uncertainty can be linked to both anxiety and depression.[6]

It makes sense: uncertainty can be unbelievably distressing. Without some sort of coping mechanism, it can impact every part of life.

I started a national charity, Knight's Cabin, that provides wellness programming and retreats for cancer survivors across Canada. When I have asked cancer patients and survivors, their number one complaint, post cancer, is the fear of recurrence.

That fear, while completely understandable, if carried around can impact every aspect of life. When I was researching what tools were available to help with the fear of recurrence, it was some form of mindfulness training. Mindfulness allows survivors (and those around them) to live in the moment, to note the fear but not react to it and to not let it cut through all aspects of life or lead to psychological distress or illness.

Looking at the big picture, if someone had a recurrence, the last thing they would want is to spend the days, months or even years living with that fear if they had a choice.

While certainly not the same, I had my own recent experience with uncertainty. When I had my first child, I developed a life-threatening complication called pre-eclampsia which forced the doctor to induce labour. My son was born (unrelated to my condition) grey and not breathing. I will never forget what it felt like laying there as they called a code blue, and I heard the team working on him repeatedly saying he was not responding for 4 minutes and

36 seconds. They airlifted medical staff from the city closest to us and he was taken away and rushed to the nearest NICU. I didn't breathe or sleep for the first six months of his life. He is now three years old and perfection.

This came back in flashes when three years later I was pregnant with my second child. Every weird pain, every fear came flooding back. The worst part was, I had so few of my usual coping mechanisms available to me (running and wine with friends). I was on bedrest for the last three months of my pregnancy, and the only way I kept my sanity when my mind started to wander to what could be was to bring myself back to the present and at least *try* to enjoy the calm before the storm.

...for Patience

They say patience is a virtue. I certainly did not inherit this virtue, and no one told me how much it would be required in life. The thing about being impatient is that you are trying to rush to the future and miss what is happening in the moment. It is the little things happening all around us that turn out to be some of the most precious in life.

Practicing mindfulness will allow you to embrace the present. The benefit to this is your own enjoyment but it is important to mention how much it will also benefit those around you. Have you ever been around an impatient person? It can be horribly annoying— they can try to finish your sentences, rush you through what you are trying to say or through decisions.

I am talking as if it is easy, but I know (as a naturally impatient person) it is not. Whether it is being stuck in traffic, waiting on medical test results, sitting through boring meetings or the never-ending requirements for patience as a parent. The worst part is, in most cases you don't have control over the situation— so you can choose to wait with a sense of anxiety and complain or you can do so calmly and even with some enjoyment of the present. The choice is yours.

As an added bonus, the times you are waiting (e.g., in line at the grocery store or in traffic) are PERFECT times to practice mindfulness or meditation.

...for Love

This section is more about building a relationship than falling in love. These two acts involve completely separate parts of the brain. Falling in love tends to turn off the parts of the brain that have rational thought and increases activity that are responsible for craving, drive and obsession.

I'll be writing about the rational part of building a long-term relationship using mindfulness. What we have to invest in our relationships is our awareness, attention, time and effort. While there are many activities to engage in to support a healthy relationship, the ability to invest your attention is certainly one of them.

Researchers have concluded that the mindfulness trait and its association to the ability and willingness to accept a partner's imperfections improved relationship satisfaction.[7] A meta-analysis (a study of all the studies) showed that a higher level of mindfulness predicted happier and more satisfying relationships (yes, please!).[8]

So how does mindfulness impact relationships? It helps us be more present and attentive. To connect with someone, you need to be able to notice when you are on autopilot—checking emails, on your phone or preoccupied with other thoughts. Mindfulness also lowers negative emotional reactivity, improves emotional regulation, can make us more empathetic and increases self-awareness. These traits are all important for successful long-term relationships.

...for Parenting

I am, by no means, an expert parent or even close. I am tripping and stumbling through every minute of it. I am learning every single day and can't begin to thank my children for what they have taught me (although, I taught them how to use a spoon, so we are even, right?). The biggest impact that mindfulness has had on my life thus far is in how I parent my children.

I have chosen a profession where I travel a lot. I am very lucky to have a husband who has a flexible job that allows him to look after our spawns while I'm on the road. I am also very grateful to have my parents nearby to help in any way they can, and my children's daycare is run by what I can only consider a saint. All of this helps with logistics. Knowing my children are in good hands and have some of the best people in the world raising them gives me incredible peace of mind. I am confident in the decision I made to pursue my career and dreams because I know that I'll be able to tell my kids: "chase your dreams like I did."

Being mindful allows me to be 100% present when I do get to spend time with them. Short amounts of time can still be quality time. Of course, this isn't true if my head is still at work, or I'm dealing with bills and trying to run the household while I'm with them. At the beginning of 2019, I travelled over 100,000 km while pregnant and incredibly ill (hyperemesis). When I got home, I was exhausted. Time with my son became a priority; my whole attention went to him.

Beyond spending quality time with your children, mindfulness also allows for you to notice the small things. Little people don't say "I had a hard day," they say, "come play with me." Being mindful helps hear the undertone of what children are asking for from their parents.

I need to reiterate: I am far from perfect at this. But I'm trying and learning every single day and, for me, this is worth every second of time practicing.

This is, of course, my specific experience. There is a lot of research being done on how mindfulness impacts parents. One of the most consistent findings is that parents who have a mindfulness meditation practice experience reduced stress, both parenting specific and generalized.[9] A parent's mindfulness practice can also help to positively impact the psychological function of their children.[10] Many aspects of decision making, such as emotional regulation during stressful situations, depends on the parent-child interactions. A parent who practices mindfulness supports the child's ability to make decisions and decreases emotional problems in the child as an adolescent.[11]

But all of this research does not help with how much I miss my children when I travel or the guilt I feel when I have to say goodbye.

While this guilt is not unique to parenting, it can be accurate in many situations. This is an example of the "mental load" that mothers carry for their families (I know there is exceptions to this, I am speaking in general). Mothers tend to be the planners, the "remember who gave the baby this outfit so they can wear it to visit them," the "before I go I made some extra meals, did the laundry and secured child care" people. Basically they are the masters of the mental to do lists. This mental load is equivalent to being CEO of the house in addition to parent and any roles served outside the home (job, volunteer, etc.). Being the keeper of so much information can be overwhelming. Mindfulness allows for disconnection when there is a moment, even if in the car between appointments or taking time off for dinner with a friend. It is ensuring that you can remain present and get the benefits from those things that you are dedicating time to.

...for Dealing with Difficult People

Wait, I already addressed this in the parenting section. Kidding!

Dealing with difficult people at work can be the most challenging aspect of many people's jobs. From difficult bosses to impossible customers, it requires a great deal of grace to be able to handle difficult people effectively day to day. The ability to respond rather than react to a situation could make all the difference in your career.

Beyond work there are the infuriating people throughout our lives—the rude call centre employee, clerks in government offices, in-laws, or three-year-olds who don't understand how it could be bedtime when everyone else is still awake. But you'll get to the results you want with everyone listed above if you can remain cool, collected and intentionally respond rather than react. No one wins when you get into a yelling match with a three-year-old. No one.

The power of our mind is that we can envision the world as it is not. I hired a property manager who was taking care of a rental property I owned. The business relationship was not working. Scratch that—it was actually horrible. He would seem to do things to get a reaction out of me. Someone suggested that when he does that, I should pretend to throw a pie in his face. It was amazing how that cooled me off and allowed me not to react. After he stopped getting a reaction out of me, he stopped trying to get under my skin with his weird conduct. While we might not always feel like we can have control over our thoughts, keeping the end goal in mind can help us avoid getting distracted by the noise along the way.

Again, as a bonus, mindfulness should also reduce the chance of *you* being a difficult person who elicits reactions in other people. It's a win-win scenario for your people skills.

...for Safety and Automatic Behaviours

Have you ever left the house and not remembered if you turned off the stove or hair straightener? Have you forgotten whether you locked the door?

Have you ever driven home, arrived in the drive-way and realized you didn't remember the drive home?

This is because these behaviours have become automatic. Our brain is secretly very lazy and likes to switch to autopilot whenever it feels like it can get away with it. Before you scold your brain, this is one way it's learned to preserve energy for behaviours we do regularly. This process, called automaticity, can free up mental resources to plan for tomorrow, remember the past, or dream up new insightful thoughts.

The problem arises when we need to remember these behaviours. For example, if you have a job that requires constant safety checks, it's probably better that they are performed with your full attention.

In order to remember and draw these behaviours to our conscious thoughts we need to become mindful (draw our attention to) these behaviours. One approach to this is to say out loud what you are doing: "I am turning off the stove." Another is to make the behaviour novel, like walking backwards towards the stove to turn it off. Both of these slight changes help draw attention to your actions and you are much more likely to remember that you have done it.

For safety checks, there are many industries now that require people to point and call out what they are doing, called very creatively the "point and call method." Tune into the flight attendants before your next flight: they are avid point and callers. This technique is most famously done by Japanese train conductors and station staff. When point and calling was introduced by the Japanese Railway Technical Research Institute, errors were reduced significantly. You might feel silly, but it's hard to argue with that kind of productivity gains.

Of course, awareness of our automatic behaviours can help with more than safety and is key to changing any behaviour and, on a much larger scale, designing the life we want.

. . . for Letting Go

One of the most profound impacts that mindfulness can have for many people is the ability to let go. Let go of fear, resentment, trauma, shame, perfectionism, etc. Letting go of what is holding you back or no longer serving you.

The ability to metaphorically put down your baggage gives you the ability to live more, be more creative, take more risks and open up yourself to possibilities. Take a second to imagine your life without the weight you have been carrying around from your past and the fears you have for your future. Pretty damn good, right? Be like Elsa from *Frozen* and let that sh!t go.

PRACTICES

Before You Start

Before you start practicing, there is one very important aspect to address. The "practice" is bringing your thoughts BACK to what you are trying to focus on—not simply noticing what you are focusing on. It is VERY NORMAL AND NATURAL to get distracted and to have thoughts pop into your head. The practice is to observe the thoughts without reacting to them, and then shift your attention back to your focus. Much like lifting some weights, this will feel laborious at first. But as you repeat the practice, your brain will get better at bringing your focus back. As with anything, some days will be better than others. Progress over perfection.

Think of yourself as a guide dog for a person who is blind. If the person wanders off course, you, without judgment, gently bring them back to the desired path.

You are the guide to your thoughts.

Embrace the distractions; they are opportunities for you to practice being a guide.

Start at your comfort level (1, 3, 5, 10 minutes?) and challenge yourself from there.

Coming to Your Senses

One of the easiest ways to quickly get your mind into the present is to come into your five senses: vision, hearing, smell, taste and touch. The idea is to move your attention as if it was a spotlight, lighting up each of the senses you are currently experiencing.

- What can you see? What colours, textures, motion, stillness?

- What can you hear? Is there a voice in the crowd carrying? Loud, abrupt noises? Something in the background?

- What do you smell? Where is the smell hitting your nose? Notice if the smell brings back memories.

- What can you taste? Is there a particular taste in your mouth?

- What are you touching? Not just your hands and fingers, are your feet rooted in the ground? Are your glutes touching the chair? How many surfaces are you touching?

This can be your practice, or you can use this to get into the present to be able to start another one of the practices. It can be helpful for people like me who struggle to direct attention to one thing at a time.

My three-year-old raises my awareness of my senses all the time. He will point up to the sky and say, "Look there is a rocket ship" (an airplane streak) or "What is that noise?" (a nearby train). It's then that I notice how unaware I am of my surroundings sometimes and hypothetically staring at my feet. Focus can be a competitive advantage, and so can noticing the world around you. Practice both.

Over a Hot Beverage

This was my first practice and this book's namesake. In my case, my drink of choice is a coffee, but of course can be done with any beverage. It is helpful to have a strong-tasting beverage that is warm (noticing the taste of water can be much too boring).

The idea is to come to your five senses, as previously described, while drinking your hot beverage.

Over an Adult Beverage a.k.a. Winefulness or Beerfulness

S peaking of strong and interesting tasting beverages, the above coffee practice can be explored in the notes of wine, beer, or your favourite hard liquor. This practice can allow you to hone in on the mindfulness skills and have more of an appreciation of the complexity, history and enjoyment of these beverages.

Can you take your time with the beverage to really experience it? This can be done by enjoying a glass slowly with a friend to add a social component. You could consider going to a wine tasting guided by a professional sommelier or a brewery tour or sampling. You can ask your friends: do you taste certain notes and flavours? Learning a bit about the history of your beverage can increase your awareness when you drink.

Mindful Walking

Remember the concept of automaticity? It's like when you walk somewhere and then realize you don't know how you got there because your brain decided to go on autopilot. Despite walking being a repetitive action, it can be a great time to incorporate mindfulness into your day.

Mindful walking is something I became passionate about when the charity I founded had an office about a twelve-minute walk from my house. I would often walk to work so deep in thought, going over my to-do list, reliving a conversation, etc., I would barely notice the world around me. Now it is worth mentioning that I live in the Rocky Mountains. My walk to work is on a path by a stream. My view, if I were only to look up, looks like a postcard. People travel from all parts of the world to see what I see every day. When I realized what I was doing, I made a conscious effort the moment I stepped outside my door to "look up." (This is also helpful while hiking to ensure you don't face plant with the unfamiliar and ever-changing terrain.)

Mindful walking can be done inside or outside, but I strongly suggest outside in nature when possible, as it adds in the health benefits of nature (explored in more detail below).

You can practice mindful walking by using your five senses to bring yourself to your environment in the present moment.

- Start by taking a moment to notice how your body feels.

- With every step, bring your awareness to the rising and falling of your feet.

- Notice when your weight shifts from one foot to the other.

- As your foot comes to the ground, notice and appreciate the support the ground gives you.

- If you do notice yourself getting distracted, just pause, notice what is distracting you and bring your attention back to your practice.

- Start to notice the sounds you can hear both near and in the distance. Any of them unusual? Have you heard the sounds before?

- Allow your mind to be still, just observe.

- What can you smell? (Hopefully it's pleasant!) Do you know the source of the smell?

- Notice your surroundings. What do you see? Look at the sky: What do you see? Is it clear?

- Reach down and touch the ground. Feel the earth, grass, rocks or whatever is on your path.

Remember, there is no right or wrong way to mindfully walk (or practice any mindfulness activities, really). Just be present and truly experience what you are doing.

In the Shower

The joke is we often shower with many people. Think of all the people you end up thinking about in the shower: your mother-in-law ("What did she mean when she said…?"), your boss ("She has unreasonable expectations") or "what's-his-name? The board's secretary. Is it Steve? I need to figure it out before today's board meeting!"

Many of us use our shower time for unconscious or conscious thoughts, whether it is a long train of unconscious thoughts or complete and non-complete thoughts to do with our past or future. Sometimes we try to use the shower time to prepare a mental to-do list.

My suggestion is this: save the to-do lists for when you actually have a pen and paper to record it. Without this, you will have to do it all over again, so it's not a productive use of your time. Instead, your shower is another opportunity to slip in a little mindfulness.

Much like how the gentle vibration of your phone is a cue to check your notifications, use turning on the water and stepping in the warm stream as a cue to become present. Vow to just shower with yourself. Come to all five senses (see exercise above) through the whole process, from preparing for the shower to stepping out and drying off.

- Where is the warm water touching you?

- What does the fresh water, body wash and shampoo smell like?

- What does it sound like when you wash?

- Do you taste anything?

- What do you see in the shower? Morning light? Different colours? Textures?

This small practice will help you start your day with some clarity and will be a small but powerful investment into your mental health. As a bonus, by not being lost in thought, you might save a little water and time from your morning shower.

Active Listening

Select a song, either one you have heard before or that you are listening to for the first time. Listen to it wearing headphones, or with decent speakers, in a noise-free environment.

Some of the following guiding practices are very sensory focused, while others require a bit more thought:

- Focus on the melody of the song and follow the inflections of either the singer's voice or the lead instrument. If you're listening to a symphony, follow the melody as it moves between sections of the orchestra.

- Pick an instrument to focus on and try to follow it for the entire song.

There are different sections in a song. The verses typically tell a story, and there are usually two or three verses. The pre-chorus usually builds the intensity of the song and leads into the chorus, which contains the main idea of the song, and usually the song's title. There's often a bridge or solo section in the last third of a song that leads into the final chorus.

- How does the energy of the song build and decline? Are new instruments introduced to increase the impact/intensity?

- What images come to your mind when you listen to the music? This may work better in a "present" sense if this is a song you haven't heard before.

- What words are being sung? How does the tone of the singer's voice heighten the power of the words?

- What words would you use to describe the tone of the singer's voice or an individual instrument?

- What emotional qualities does the song have?

There are more questions and points of focus that could work for Active Listening. You could also take similar questions and do Active Watching. While watching your favourite TV show/movie can you become more engaged with the content?

The above practice was suggested by Peter Vooys, an elementary music teacher. He told me that "this practice is something that I'm in the process of working out with my students, but my personal use of it has been enriching to my life for many years."

Breathing

You can meditate by placing focus on all sorts of things: the shower, scenery while walking, your adult beverage. Your breath, however, is one very powerful way to focus your attention, as its conveniently with you all the time. Noticing and controlling your breath can be the most powerful tool to decrease stress and anxiety and allow your mind to focus when it needs to the most. It is both a useful tool as a daily practice and in the moments of acute stress. By breathing deeply, you change the levels of oxygen and carbon dioxide in your bloodstream and trick your brain into thinking that it's less anxious that it actually is. As a result, you can get an almost immediate calming effect, both physically and psychologically.

One of the simplest forms of breathing exercises to reduce stress and anxiety is one of the first things that a psychologist (or other mental health professional) will teach you. It is simple and very effective.

Breathe in for a 4 count and out for an 8 count.

For more breathing exercises visit www.consciousworks.co/cup-of-mindfulness

Here is a breathing practice that many people I work with enjoy.

Box Breathing

This practice is also known as *battle breathing* or *bomb breathing*, because...well...this is an exercise they teach people who are going into battle or who disengage bombs. It controls our stress response so that people can remain calm enough to take the shot with accuracy, make informed decisions (responding instead of reacting) and stay controlled enough in the intricate and immensely stressful work of disengaging a bomb.

This breathing pattern immediately engages your parasympathetic nervous system (the system responsible for bringing you back to a calm state) to help control your physiological stress (i.e., rapid heartbeat, shaking hands, dry mouth) and help you to focus your attention on your desired activity in order to perform it well.

Using the breath to calm the mind and body needs to be practiced in order to have it available to you in the times you really need it. The idea is to be able to kick into this breathing without continuously counting so you can perform the task at hand.

For this practice, each 4 count is slow and equal to the next.

Breathe in for 4, 3, 2, 1

Hold your breath for 4, 3, 2, 1

Breathe out for 4, 3, 2, 1

Hold your breath out for 4, 3, 2, 1

It helps with the stress and performance of people who DISENGAGE BOMBS! I am confident it can help, at least a little, with most of your daily stresses.

This graphic is also included at the back of the book to cut out and place somewhere where you can use a cue to practice. For some people that will be in the car to remind them to practice while they are in traffic, on a teenager's door to remind them to engage in the breathing before interactions, in your office to remind you to practice in between meetings or on a bathroom mirror to start the day off with the practice.

Breath work doesn't need to be complicated. Any time you observe the breath it will slow and become deeper without any effort. What is almost magical about breathing practices is that it can give you what you need in a particular situation. When you are sluggish, focusing on the breath can give you energy. When you are anxious, some deliberate breathing can calm the mind and body.

Left Big Toe

You can meditate on anything. What I mean by that is that you can draw your awareness to anything in your environment, for example, a candle, snowflakes falling, your newborn's face. The idea is that you practice drawing your attention to that one thing. It is practicing your focus, meaning if you get distracted, you bring your attention back to whatever you are focusing on.

What I use is my left big toe. Why? Well, I have it with me all the time. As you read this, pause and think of your left big toe. Just your toe. Try this for a minute.

Are you able to focus on your toe? Was this challenging? Did your thoughts wander? Were you able to bring your attention back to your toe?

I love this practice because it is a demonstration of not being able to think about two things concurrently. If you are able to focus on your left big toe, you are unable to think or worry about anything else. Again, the particular benefit of this practice is you have your left big toe with you at all times. I have used this practice often to get through events, or to simply catch my thoughts as they start racing away from me.

An example, when I was thirty-two years old, I had the impossible task of giving my best friend's eulogy. This is one of the most emotionally provoking situations I can think of and yet, I knew I had to say the words. I cannot tell you how many hours I spent writing and re-writing to sum up a beautiful life and friendship. I speak publicly for a living: the thought of a stage and an audience was not an issue. It was the emotion. The indescribable loss, sadness, fear, frustration, trauma and grief on top of absolutely no sleep. But I had to say the words.

As I sat there, listening to the speakers before me, all I could think about was my big toe. I was very aware I had to feel all the feelings at some point, but now was not the time. I had to say the words. I walked up, LEFT BIG TOE. I saw her high school boyfriend in the audience, LEFT BIG TOE. Her mom nodding her head to agree with my words, LEFT BIG TOE.

Through the whole day, I LEFT TOED the sh!t out of it. I remain eternally grateful to my toe for getting me through the impossible and being able to get the words out when I needed to.

I was giving a keynote speech and used this practice. I had NO idea how the talk was going and did not get as much feedback as I am used to getting from the audience. After I left, I checked Twitter and #leftbigtoe was trending. I believe it went well.

A couple of weeks later an audience member from that talk emailed me. He said it was such a simple practice he taught it to his eight-year-old son who has anxiety to help him fall asleep. He had incredible success.

Never underestimate the power of a very simple practice…and your left big toe.

In Your Environment

Similar to the Left Big Toe practice, you can pick something in your environment to focus on. Examples could be something like a candle, snowflakes as they fall, the sound of the rain, waves crashing or music. Focus on something specific, when your thoughts wander, simply guide them back to your object of focus.

This allows you to appreciate the world around you. It is a practice I use especially when I travel that brings me to the present and helps me enjoy my new environment.

Mindful Eating

"We overeat, not because we enjoy food too much,
it is because we don't enjoy it enough"
- Charles Eisenstein

Many of us eat food mindlessly. We are too preoccupied with watching TV, working, or driving to notice or appreciate what we are consuming. This type of eating is less satisfying and can lead to overeating without realizing what we're doing.

A common and incredible practice that dieticians use to introduce this concept is to slowly eat a raisin (or really any small piece of food—my favourite is good quality, dark chocolate) and do the Come to Your Senses exercise.

Many people are amazed with how much flavour and texture food can have. Practice chewing your food slowly and paying attention, even when you are eating on the run, to have a more satisfying eating experience and increase your enjoyment of the food with the added bonus of being able to digest the food better. As much as possible, avoid other activities such as watching TV, reading or working while eating.

To take mindfulness eating a step further, you can bring awareness without judgment to all aspects of your eating habits. This helps people who over or under consume food and emotional eaters to better understand conscious and unconscious decisions made around food.

This method is largely taking the place of traditional nutrition management that focused on the what and how much someone ate without considering aspects of our eating habits.

Progressive Muscle Relaxation

I find this technique particularly beneficial to help me sleep. I like to practice this if I am feeling anxious or restless when I get into bed. I often have a very hard time sleeping—either getting to sleep or waking in the middle of the night—if I have a flight the next day or an early morning meeting. After I get the tension out of my muscles, I start to practice a breathing technique. This practice has been a saviour!

The idea is simple enough: tense and relax your muscles in a particular order. Focus on tensing the muscles as much as you comfortably can and fully letting go. When you think you cannot let go any more, relax further.

- Start with your toes and feet. While inhaling, contract all the muscles in your toes and feet for 5–10 seconds, then exhale suddenly releasing the tension in that muscle group.

- Give yourself 10 seconds to completely relax before moving on to the next muscle group (calves).

- When you are relaxing the muscles, imagery may help. Imagine the stress flowing out of your muscles.

- Progress up your body to the different muscle groups. When you get to your head, make sure you contract your facial muscles and your jaw. They often hold a lot of tension.

INTEGRATING INTO YOUR LIFE

Adding in the Elements
and Getting into Nature

There is no doubt of the health benefits of nature. This is why nature is being used more and more to both prevent and treat illness. For example, forest bathing is already a popular treatment in Japan. Forest bathing has absolutely nothing to do with bathing in a forest, but rather it involves people mindfully spending time in the forest either sitting, lying down or walking around. There is something almost magical about the combination of natural environments and mindfulness, which scientists are now trying to understand.

Researchers gathered evidence from over 140 studies that included over 290 million people to explore the impact of nature on health. The study revealed that it can impact the immediate stress response to improve mood, reduce blood pressure, decrease heart rate, relieve muscle tension and even the production of stress hormones. Furthermore, living close to or spending time in nature can also significantly reduced the risk of Type II diabetes, cardiovascular disease, premature death and preterm births and even help us sleep better at night.[12]

As a result of these reported health benefits, we are seeing nature therapy being explored for a host of other conditions, from PTSD in soldiers, to cancer survivors, and even mental health conditions such as depression and anxiety. How does simply immersing yourself in nature achieve all of these health bonuses?

As we have discussed, our attention plays an important role in how we learn, make decisions and generally process information. When our attention is fatigued, it can impact nearly every aspect of life. Our brains can need time to recover. In line with evolutionary perspectives, a return to our natural environments can facilitate this recovery.[13] Many aspects of nature automatically draw our attention, which can mindfully bring us to the present moment with less effort. One study suggests that this might be because brain networks responsible for mind-wandering and focused attention become uncoupled. The end result is that compared to being in a city, it's easier to be mindful beside a stream, on top of a mountain, in the middle of the desert or even in a well-designed city park.[14]

In a study I am currently conducting, we explored how people take breaks during work hours. I found that while almost all breaks are beneficial or neutral (the one exception is social media breaks) for performance and mental health, breaks that included a nature component significantly improved both performance and mental health. In short, add nature into your breaks to recharge your capacity to be mindful.

Similar to breaks, exercise in general has a positive effect on health and performance including creativity, productivity, focus, etc. If you add the element of nature, dubbed *green exercise*, you amplify both effects of nature and of physical activity.[15]

While scientists are actively studying the benefits of nature, we don't yet have a complete understanding of why nature has such an extensive impact on our brains. Some people think it's simply about getting a break, others think it has to do with the body's recovery from stress, while others still think it's about the brain's recovery of attention. More than likely it is a combination of all of the above.

In summary, nature has a profound impact; it guides our brains into a state of recovery and aids in our ability to manage our attention.

What Does Technology Have to Do with It?

Technology is incredible and allows us to connect and do more than ever before. It can, however, have a negative impact on our health. In order to have a healthy relationship with technology, mindfulness can aid in navigating the interaction.

Many of the most popular uses of technology: Google, YouTube, Netflix and other streaming sites, and all social media sites HAVE NO END! They have been developed to lead you to the next and the next and the next interaction. As soon as you are done one show or movie on a streaming service the next one is queued up and ready to go. Find the end of your Facebook feed—I dare you!

As previously mentioned, part of what I study is how we take breaks, more specifically how could we take more effective breaks. Most breaks are good for us and we receive a positive benefit for our performance and psychological well-being. However, when we mindlessly consume content, it has a negative impact.

So, do you think Netflix is a good way to recover from a hard day?

Yes and no.

If you come home after a hard day, grab some delicious food, and line up a movie or a couple of shows you love, even get someone you enjoy to watch it with you, then it is a great way to end a stressful day. You are consciously consuming the content.

But if you sit down on the sofa and "let Netflix watch you" as in, absent mindedly watch whatever the algorithm selects for you, that has a negative impact on your psychological health.[16]

I thought I had a healthy relationship to technology and would have argued with anyone who would have claimed differently until I was invited to a conference about disconnection taking place in the middle of nowhere. I am talking a drive into the Canadian wilderness, then taking a helicopter trip the rest of the way. No cell service, no wifi.

Would the thought of being disconnected for three days excite you or cause you anxiety?

It was -40. Outhouses only. I learned a lot about myself over the three days.

What I did when we landed surprised me. Dressed in the warmest clothes I had—I am talking parka and snow pants—I ran under the rotors of the helicopter and when I was standing waiting for the rest of the passengers, I CHECKED MY

CELLPHONE! Why? It was basically a high-tech brick at this point and further to that I was willing to take off my mitt to do it. Checking my phone was so habitual, I even did it when I consciously knew there was no chance of communication.

Using my cellphone is now something I try to take off of autopilot. I'm much more conscious with my phone—leaving it at the door, trying not to have my phone next to me as I sleep and leaving it home for dates with my husband or walks with friends.

In short, consumed consciously, technology can aid and ease our daily lives. However, if we slip into unconscious consumption it can negatively impact our moods, health and relationship.

One Thing at a Time

I am a great multi-tasker.

annoying sound that indicates you are wrong

Many people do multiple things at once, but this does not mean they are good at it.

As humans we CANNOT multi-task things that require any amount of real effort. Can you watch Netflix and fold laundry? Sure. Or drive and talk to the passenger? Sure. Because these activities have started to be automatic and habitual taking very little cognitive power to implement. Next time you're driving with a friend and the weather turns real sour, real quick, watch how much the conversation drops so you can give the focus demanded from the road.

Can you...and I am about to ruin some relationships here...text and listen to the person in front of you? NO!

The human brain can only do one cognitively heavy/novel task at a time. When we *think* we are multi-tasking, we are actually switching between two or more tasks very quickly. Turns out, every time we switch tasks, the brain needs to take a moment to reset for the new task. This results in multi-tasking often being more effortful and more time consuming. Or you just completely fail at one of the tasks. Have you ever accidentally started texting what you were saying or speaking what you were just trying to type? Mini experiment: Try typing and having a conversation at the same time. Have someone check how well you do.

The benefit of mindfulness is to be able to focus on doing one thing at a time. This lets you do more with the brain power that you have and more with every minute you have. Even more importantly, mindfulness allows you to notice when you are distracted or attempting to do multiple things at once and will allow you to bring yourself back to what you CHOOSE to put your attention towards; this could be time with kids, tackling your work tasks, or soaking in the glory of a winefulness session with friends.

While avoiding multi-tasking can have a measurable impact on your performance, productivity and time management skills, I've notice this has had the most impact on my relationships. I notice when someone provides me with undivided attention (mainly because it is so rare) and I'm able to return the favour. It's lovely and I suggest practicing it within your social world.

Example of a practice: when you get home from work (or over breakfast or whenever works for you) have a conversation with your partner (friend, child) and do absolutely nothing else. Lean into the conversation (literally with active listening skills), have eye contact, ask questions, nod and completely engage. Phone out of reach and sight. Simple. Meaningful. Impactful.

Attention Is Our Currency

Think of your attention like a flashlight that is able to point in the direction you would like to go and can shine either a concentrated area with a strong beam or widen the focus to make a larger field of light and to take in more information. Mindfulness (or attention management) helps you both shoot the light in the direction you would like to go, focusing specifically on one thing (e.g., writing a report) and control how wide the light is (e.g., being able to perform a task safely and take into account other risks such as on a construction site). Imaging how this light would look if you were stumbling home drunk; this is what your attention is like without mindfulness.

It is important to note that your time and energy get invested wherever your attention is set. If you are not conscious about your attention, you are spending your most valuable assets (time and energy) recklessly and probably wasting them.

Try taking a day where you consciously notice where your time and energy are going or even take a step further and record when your mind is wandering. Challenge yourself: Is your time being spent towards your goals? Towards your most valued relationships? Towards your passions?

Don't get me wrong: being bored and daydreaming have their place and can be incredibly useful for everything from time to time. While I did earlier challenge you to take mindful showers, how many people also acknowledge having great ideas while in the shower? The goal is not necessarily to be conscious of your attention, your whole existence, and never let the mind wander. Instead, creativity, innovation and general well-being can all be boosted when you can allocate attention effectively when you want. Can you be conscious with your attention when you need to be?

Make It a Damn Habit

"Mindfulness isn't difficult. We just need to remember to do it." —Sharon Salzberg

The actual act of meditation or mindfulness practices are not particularly difficult: it's just focusing on your breath or something like that. It's *remembering* to practice that can be challenging, however.

In order to make small mindfulness practices part of your daily behaviour it is best to establish them as a habit. In order to do so, we need to understand the anatomy of a habit: a cue, the behaviour and the reward.

Anatomy of a Habit

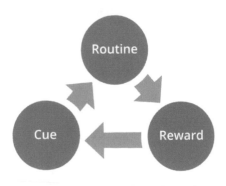

For your mindfulness behaviour, choose a cue. This is something that prompts the initiation of the behaviour. The most efficient way to develop a sustainable habit is to pick a cue that is a "keystone habit," a habit you perform every day regardless of your situation or location. In other words, what are some habits you perform even during incredible stressful periods or while you are travelling? Some examples could be brushing your teeth, drinking coffee in the morning, arriving to your office in the morning or eating breakfast.

Anchor your new habit (e.g., mindfulness practice) by doing it very close in time to your pre-established routine or keystone habits. As an example, I will put the coffee machine on and practice mindfulness until the pot is done or water is boiled, or I will practice mindfulness for ten minutes immediately after my alarm goes off in the morning. Many leaders I know sit in their driveway or garage and practice a mindfulness activity for a few minutes after driving home from work. It allows them to separate home from work and become present with their families.

In addition to anchoring your practices in keystone habits, you can set reminders to be mindful into your phone or leave Post-it notes where you'll see them (on the mirror, on the coffee pot). Imagine if you could slip in a little mindfulness practice every time you check your phone. You would be so Zen.

Other reminders can be people. For example, get someone to hold you accountable. This can be done by going to a meditation class or find a friend or family member to support or remind you. My friend and I decided to challenge each other to meditating for five to ten minutes a day for a month. After each session we would text each other proof of our session. It kept us on track. And while we did not have a flawless record the entire month (I skipped a couple days due to various reasons), we certainly practiced more than if left on our own.

The reward for the activity must be meaningful and immediately following the mindfulness session. I often hear things such as "I will buy myself a new shirt after I meditate/practice mindfulness for 2 weeks." This could work, but it probably won't.

The reward isn't close enough to the practice, so they never become linked in your brain. Also, due to its material nature, I would advise against this reward set up. One of the best reward systems (and why social media is so incredibly popular and addictive) is social validation (a thumbs up if you will). Again, one of the reasons my friend and I had such success in the month of meditation is we would praise each other and offer a literal thumbs up when complete. An excellent reward can be a high five from a spouse, joining a social media mindfulness practice group or giving your friends a gold star sticker when it is complete.

No Pass/Fail

Progress over perfection. Always.

One of the most common mistakes made when starting a new habit is this idea of pass/fail thinking, especially for high performers. Behaviours are hard to change and new habits hard to develop; we have to be kind to ourselves and patient.

Often I will hear people say things such as "I will start running every morning at 6 a.m." But then something in life gets in the way—illness, travel, work, etc. The person misses one, two or several days and then it's "well, I guess I failed" or "I guess I am not a runner."

Could you imagine if we spoke to children like that? When a baby is learning to walk, we make all these ridiculous noises and encourage every attempt with such love, support and countless opportunities to try again. Just imagine how heartbreaking it would be to treat our kid's journey to walking like our journey to mindfulness?

"Come on [baby's name] you got this! One foot in front of the other" (said in a high pitched, encouraging voice).

They fall.

"Well, I guess you are not a walker."

Instead, imagine if we took the same approach with ourselves as we did with our little bundles of joy. The same love, encouragement, and compassion should be used on ourselves as we try to develop a new behaviour. Simple changes in the language that we use when talking about ourselves, such as changing *fail* into *not yet*, can increase our odds of attempting the behaviour again. Remember, mindfulness is not a sprint, but a lifelong marathon of practice.

The idea of "not yet" has such incredible power. It is literally the fabled "growth mindset" summarized into two words. It communicates that there is a learning curve and success is not black or white.

A particularly profound example is that of a high school where many of their students were failing their classes. The administration decided to put *not yet* on their report cards instead of *fail*. The students were significantly more likely to retake the course.

6

CONCLUSION

Conclusion of Airport Purgatory

Back to my story of being trapped in Pearson Airport with no money and ID. Did I get on my plane?

I did. Being able to remain calm and present allowed me to think through all the information I had. Think of the flashlight example: I was able to focus my light field to take in all the relevant information. What I did have was my laptop...and on that laptop was saved a copy of our passports from a few years ago while we were travelling in Europe. Based on that, and after answering an extensive list of questions about the booking, I was able to get on the flight.

Life Lesson: always have a cloud version (well protected, of course) of important documents #scanyourpassport

They did warn me though, that while I could get to St. John's, Newfoundland, I would not be able to get on my return flight without ID. This was slightly concerning as I had a commitment first thing on the day after I was to fly back. The agents left a note for my husband to send my information as soon as he landed in Calgary. Given that Canada is such a large country, there is no overnight mailing—it takes two days. This left me following around a UPS truck before going into a rural area for the cancer retreat I was hosting.

I approached the UPS delivery guy. I told him my story and he said "No problem. I can give you the package, I just need to see your ID."

....

Funny story. My ID is *IN* the package. Thankfully my husband had added my host's name to the package. I got my IDs, got on the plane and returned in time for my speaking engagement.

In conclusion, I was able to get on the plane and get my wallet back and I owe it all to my mindful cups of coffee. The small practice of consciously bringing myself to my five senses over my morning cup of coffee allowed me to have a greater understanding of where my attention was going and to bring it back to what I wanted to focus on. In this situation, the practice allowed me to be able to focus on the goal at hand and cast my attention on the necessary information I would need to get onto that plane.

Now What?

Mindfulness is one of the most effective ways to take care of your brain, mental health, and performance.

You will see the results of a short mindfulness practice in almost every aspect of life, from your closest relationship to dealing with the most challenging situations life throws at you.

We practice mindfulness so that it will kick in when we need it. Just like when we practice a sport (or instrument, or big speech) we repeat the practice so that by game day it is automatic.

The first step is figuring out how a short practice can be integrated into your life so that it can exist even in the busiest, most chaotic times (a.k.a. when you need it the most). When you do get a moment, get curious and expand your practice, try a different practice, try an app or a course.

This book is meant to be an introduction. Try the practices. What works in your life? Where is your attention being spent? What happens if you become more conscious with your thoughts and pay attention to where you are spending your energy and time? Take note and celebrate the small changes.

For further resources and practices visit www.consciousworks.co/cup-of-mindfulness

REFERENCES

1. Killingsworth, M. A., & Gilbert, D. T. (2010). A wandering mind is an unhappy mind. *Science, 330*(6006), 932.

2. Norris, C. J., Creem D., Hendler R., & Kober, H. (2018). Brief mindfulness meditation improves attention in novices: Evidence from ERPs and moderation by neuroticism. *Frontier Human Neuroscience, 12,* 315.

3. Hedden, T., Gabrieli, J. (2004). Insights into the ageing mind: A view from cognitive neuroscience. *Nat Rev Neurosci, 5,* 87–96 doi:10.1038/nrn1323

4. Luders, E., Cherbuin, N., & Gaser, C. (2016). Estimating brain age using high-resolution pattern recognition: Younger brains in long-term meditation practitioners. *NeuroImage, 134,* 508–513. http://www.neuro.uni-jena.de/pdf-files/Luders-NI16.pdf

5. Huang, F., Hsu, A., Hsu, L., Tsai, J., Huang, C., Chao, Y., Hwang, T., & Wu C. W. (2019). Mindfulness improves emotion regulation and executive control on bereaved individuals: An fMRI study. *Frontier Human Neuroscience, 12,* 541.

6. Nekić, M., & Mamić, S. (2019). Intolerance of uncertainty and mindfulness as determinants of anxiety and depression in female students. *Behav Sci (Basel), 9*(12), 135 doi: 0.3390/bs9120135

7. Kappen, G., Karremans, J. C., Burk, W. J., & Buyukcan-Tetik, A. (2018). On the association between mindfulness and romantic relationship satisfaction: the role of partner acceptance. *Mindfulness, 9*(5), 1543–1556.

8. McGill J., Adler-Baeder F., & Rodriguez P. (2016). Mindfully in love: A meta-analysis of the association between mindfulness and relationship satisfaction. *Journal of Human Sciences and Extension, 4*(1), 89–101.

9. Corthorn, C. (2018). Benefits of mindfulness for parenting in mothers of preschoolers in Chile. *Frontier Psychology,* 9:1443 https://doi.org/10.3389/fpsyg.2018.01443; Burgdorf, V., Szabo, M. & Abbott, M. J. (2019). The effect of mindfulness interventions for parents on parenting stress and youth psychological outcomes: A systematic review and meta-analysis. *Frontier Psychology, 10,* 1336 doi: 10.3389/fpsyg.2019.01336.

10. Burgdorf, V., Szabo, M. & Abbott, M. J. (2019). The effect of mindfulness interventions for parents on parenting stress and youth psychological outcomes: A systematic review and meta-analysis. *Frontier Psychology, 10,* 1336 doi: 10.3389/fpsyg.2019.01336

11. Wong, K., Hicks, L. M., Seuntjens, T. G., Trentacosta, C. J., Hendriksen, T. H. G., Zeelenberg, M., & van den Heuvel, M. I. (2019). The role of mindful parenting in individual and social decision-making in children. *Frontier Psychology,* (10) 550 https://doi.org/10.3389/fpsyg.2019.00550; Wang, Y., Liang, Y., Fan, L., Lin, K., Xie, X., Pan, J., & Zhou, H. (2018). The indirect path from mindful parenting to emotional programs in adolescents: The role of maternal warmth and adolescents' mindfulness. *Frontier Psychology, 9,* 546 doi: 10.3389/fpsyg.2018.00546.

12. Twohig-Bennett, C. & Jones, A. (2018). The health benefits of the great outdoors: A systematic review and meta-analysis of greenspace exposure and health outcomes. *Environmental Research, 166,* 628-637.

13. Kaplen, S. (September 1995). The restorative benefits of nature: Toward an integrative framework. *Journal of Environmental Psychology, 15*(3), 169–182.

14. Van Praag, C. D. G., Garfinkel, S. N., Sparasci, O., Mees, A., Philippides, A. O., Ware, M., Ottaviani, C. & Critchley, H. D. (2017). Mind-wandering and alterations to default mode network connectivity when listening to naturalistic versus artificial sounds. *Scientific Reports, 7,* 45273 doi: 10.1038/srep45273

15. Atchley, R. A., Strayer, D. L., & Atchley, P. (2012). Creativity in the wild: Improving creative reasoning through immersion in natural settings. *PloS one, 7*(12), https://doi.org/10.1371/journal.pone.0051474

16. Hasan, M. R., Jha, A. K. & Lui, Y. (2018). Excessive use of online video streaming services: Impact of recommender system use, psychological factors and motives. *Computer in Human Behaviour, 80,* 220–228.

Dr. Lisa Bélanger

Dr. Lisa Bélanger is the CEO of ConsciousWorks, a consulting company that shows leaders and teams how insights from behavioural science can be applied in the workplace to optimize the performance, productivity, and innovation with clients that span the globe. She helps close the gap between intention and action resulting in long-term change and a competitive advantage.

Photo: Alexis McKeown

Dr. Bélanger is also a Certified Exercise Physiologist, researcher at the University of Calgary, instructor at the University of Alberta Executive Education, and the author of *Inspire Me Well: Finding Motivation to Take Control of Your Health*. Additionally, she is the founder of Knight's Cabin, a national charity offering no-cost wellness programming to cancer survivors.

Her most notable accomplishments are running the Paris marathon, climbing Kilimanjaro and creating two tiny humans. You can find her working with her portable desk at the top of the mountain at home in Canmore, Alberta, or another corner of the world. When she is not working, she is most likely on her way to yoga, out for a run or taste testing the local coffee and wine.

Box Breathing

Breathe in for 4, 3, 2, 1

Hold your breath for 4, 3, 2, 1

Breathe out for 4, 3, 2, 1

Hold your breath out for 4, 3, 2, 1

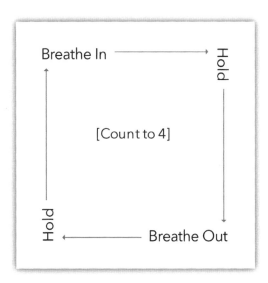